MOLONEY
UP
AND
AT IT

First published in 1984 by Mercier Press
PO Box 5, 5 French Church Street, Cork and 16 Hume Street Dublin 2
This edition 1995

ISBN 1 85635 129 7

10 9 8 7 6 5 4 3 2 1

A CIP record for this title is available from the British Library

Cover design by Niamh Sharkey
Set by Richard Parfrey
Printed in Ireland by ColourBooks, Baldoyle Industrial Estate, Dublin 13

MOLONEY
UP
AND
AT IT

BRENDAN
KENNELLY

MERCIER PRESS

Contents

MOLONEY
UP
AND
AT IT

My soul from hell, the night the ould wan died,
Moloney said, I cried an' cried
Tears down. I'd been tied to her string
Through rack and hardship and the wild fling
O' youth, through manhood and the grey
Days when youth begins to slip away,
And now my addled heart and head
Were bound by the memory of the dead.

Well, anyway, after puttin' herself down
In the box, I went to the town
O' Lishtowel for a few drinks, and there
I met a Knockanore woman with red hair
And gamey eye. I made bold
And in short time had told
Her my story. She cocked her ear and listened well.
We drank until the darkness fell
And for hours after. The talk
Spun on love. 'Can I walk
A piece with you?' says I. 'Moloney,' says she,
'You're welcome to do what you like with me.'
Fair enough! We left Lishtowel and struck the road,
Footin' it free over pothole
And gravel. The Knockanore woman was full o' guff
And harped on all the tricks o' love.
I upped with my question. She
Was willin' and free.
'Where would you like it?' says I. 'Well,' she said,
'God's green earth is a warm bed.'

'Right you are, girl,' says I.
It happened we were passin' by
Gale graveyard where my mother lay.
'What would you say
To this place?' says I. 'Moloney,' says she,
'If it's right with you, it's right with me.'

Straightaway, I opened the gate and led
The Knockanore woman over the dead
O' seven parishes. Talk of a flyer!
Fasht as they come an' hot as fire!
She fell down on the soft clay
Of a fresh grave, and before I could say
A word, I was on the ground as well,
Goin' like the hammers o' hell!
'Twas only then I saw where I was.
On my mother's grave! But that was no cause
For panic, though I was a bit
Upset at first by the strangeness of it.
The Knockanore woman was happy as Larry,
And I was sparkin' and merry
As a cricket. 'Yerra, you might
As well enjoy the gift o' the night
While you have the chance,' I said
To myself, realisin' the dead are dead,
Past holiness, and harms -
And the livin' woman was in my arms.

'Twas great fun
While it lasted, and it lasted long. The sun
Was startin' to climb the sky when we rose
Up and settled our clothes.
'How are you, girl?' says I.
'Yerra, fine,' says she.
''Twas a fine night,' says I.
''Twas so, but a bit cold towards mornin',' says she,
'And I wouldn't mind a hot cup o' tay
This minute.' 'You're a wise woman,' I said,
'Let them say whatever they say,
There's wan thing sure. 'Tis hard to bate the cup o' tay.'
And then, 'Whisht,' I said,
Suddenly remembering the quiet dead.
With the memory, I started to sing,
Then and there, a bar of a jig,
And as I sang I danced as well
On the body whose soul was in heaven or hell.
'You're a gay man,' says she, 'to bring
Me to a place like this for your bit of a fling,
And I'm thinkin' the love has gone to your head
When you dance a jig on the bones o' the dead.'
Said I, 'By the Christ that is divine,
If I have a son may he dance on mine.
While a man has the chance he should dance and sing,'
    I said,
'For he'll be the hell of a long time dead.
So come on now without further ado
And I'll put on the kettle for the tay.'

She smiled and we started on our way
In the early light that was breakin' for day.

The night was lost, the daylight stretched ahead,
Behind me slept the unforgettable dead,
Beside me stepped a woman with gamey eye,
Laughin' as the sun mounted the sky.

MOLONEY
AT THE
WAKE

That was a gay night, he said,
    I went to a wake and hopped into bed
With the corpse; not a very nice
Thing to do, I suppose; cold as ice
Her belly and thighs;
Two brown pennies covered her eyes;
They'd tied up her foxy hair
And crossed her hands as though in prayer.
When alive, the same girl wasn't much
Given to prayers and such,
But they made her look as though she could
Have prayed the legs from under God.
Anyway, I got into bed
There and then beside the dead
Woman; a disastrous
Thing to do because the whole house
Thought I was mad. I drew a long
Breath, looked at her and broke into song.
With her icy belly against my knee
I sang 'Old girl, why don't you answer me?'
Christ, man, talk of a scatter! The whole place
Panicked; 'tis a terrible disgrace,
They said, when a drunken sot the like o' you
Can stagger in here through
The open door, and without an attempt at a prayer
Make a wild buck-lepp in there
Beside herself, and she stretched.
            Never mind, I said,
What do you, or I, know of the dead?

Of course, I grant that politeness must be shown
At all times, so I'll get up now and leave her alone.
Two mugs o' porter, a quick *Hail Mary* for the dead,
Then I hit for home and the wife in bed.
I was glad to see her, she to see me,
We were both as livin' as we needed to be
To do as our bodies prayed us to do.
When the soul is a liar, the body is true.
A body is all a poor man has got
And love is a moment before we rot.
Moloney smiled and lifted his glass:
'Tis a privilege to drink to all things that pass.'

MOLONEY
MEETS
MISS
IMMACULATA
MULLALLY

The minute I looked at her, Moloney said,
I knew the woman was bored in her bones.
And why wouldn't she be,
In the name of all that's holy?
There she was, slavin' away
In the spotless kitchen of the priests' presbytery,
Day in, day out, without break, complaint or fuss.
The reason I was in that house
Was to get a priest for a man
Who was dead already
So I wasn't in too big of a hurry.
It makes me laugh to think
What the livin' believe
They can do for the dead
With prayers an' fuss an' holy oils
An' fine words for their souls.

'What's your name, girl,' I said,
Thinkin' to lift the boredom from her.
'Immaculata Mullally,' she replied.
'That's a great job you have,' I said,
'Lookin' after the holy priests
While they look after the sinful world.'
'Well,' she said, ''Tis all right as jobs go
But there's other things I'd rather do.'
And she winked, I think.

May God be thanked for women's winks,
They often say what a man thinks

But lacks the heart to tell.
One wink is as good as two tongues.
　'Immaculata,' I said, 'I know well
How you feel. It must break
Your heart to have to make
Breakfast, dinner and supper,
Spring, summer, autumn an' winter
For the parish priest an' his careful curate.
Even on Sunday you don't get a rest.
In fact, that must be the worst
Day o' the week for you
With two starvin' men to feed
At different times o' the day.
Heavenly fartin' father,' I said,
'Have you ever stood
Back from yourself, Immaculata, an' seen
The way you're wastin' the cream
O' your womanhood on the holy men:
Up on your feet at the crack o' dawn,
Always havin' to put a nice face on
For every bollox that comes to the door,
Drunk an' sober, rich an' poor,
Every tinkery Dick an' Harry
Seekin' confession or permission to marry,
Wantin' the priest by day an' night
To baptise a child or anoint an eejit.
'Tis a wonder you're not driven out o' your wits.
Immaculata,' I said, 'If the truth were known
A priest's housekeeper is a martyr born

An' if you're not careful, a martyr's fate
In the heel o' the hunt is what you'll get,
The perfect servant of every fool
Thinkin' to keep his soul from hell.
Why are these people so afraid?
Why do they live like men half-dead?
What's in their eyes when they come to your door?
God gave them life but they want more.
No, no, not more but less,' I said,
'Do you live in the world of the half-dead,
Miss Mullally, and is there where you want to be?'

   When I spoke these words to her, I knew
I would lie on her belly in no time at all,
Happy as Adam before his fall.
An' sure enough
We made love
On the kitchen floor o' the priest's house,
Shiny an' polished an' quiet an' nice.
From start to finish, our love was good
An' herself an' myself enjoyed
Every bit of it. Afterwards
Her eyes were kind,
She gave me a glass o' whiskey
From the priest's bottle
An' I can tell you
That was as good a drop
As I ever had in all my natural
Days and nights as a drinkin' man.

I was right for another drink when in
Strode the parish priest, Father Bob McGlynn.

'Well, my good man,' he said, 'And what
Can I do for you?'
'A man that's dead,' I said, 'Is in need of a priest
Though there's little enough
You can do for him now.'
'Leave that to me,' snapped Father McGlynn,
'Perhaps I can clean his soul of sin
Even at this late hour.'
'Maybe you can,' I said, 'For 'tis you have the power
While the likes o' myself, a simple man,
Must be grateful to God for all he can
Find an' keep from day to day.
Of one thing only a poor man is sure,
To refuse what God offers is the way to be poor.'

'Quite so,' he smiled. 'Well, lead the way
Before it gets dark.
I must be about the good Lord's work.'

'Father,' I said, 'We won't delay
A second longer. The light o' day
Is on my side
So gather your gear for the house o' the dead
Because that's where you're wanted now.'

As I opened the door I turned my head.

'Thank you, Miss Mullally,' I said.

MOLONEY'S
REVENGE

The Lover Flynn, Moloney said,
  Was a gay man, accordin' to many. He'd
Go through women like shit through a goose.
Through the length an' breadth of the land he was
Famous for capers. The gas
Thing was he didn't give a fiddler's fart
For any woman, though chasin', in worst and best,
The delights of belly, bum and breast.
Came the day, Moloney said,
When he coaxed a woman out of my bed
And treated her like all the others,
Leavin' me high and dry, like many another mother's
Son. That was the Lover out the door -
He'd take the lot and come back for more
And never give a tinker's curse
What soul was wounded, what body was hurt,
What heart-breakin' things were said or done.
The Lover was gone, a shot from a gun.

  But every dog will have his day
And the time will come, come what may,
When the man who has broken many a heart
Will lose his own, and the craft and art
Of years can't help him. So it was
With the Lover Flynn. He fell
Arseoverappetite headoverheels in love
With the tidiest thing you ever saw.
A doctor's daughter, neat an' prim,
Halted the gallop of the Lover Flynn.

Now a man in love is a man gone mad
And the Lover wanted to prove he had
Talent and brains and money galore;
If she asked for something, he'd give her more
And more again. The day arrived
When the Lover at last decided
He'd try to take her for a wife
And settle down in the married life.
As you well know, my friends, there's no-one more
Respectable than your unscrupulous fucker
When he decides to settle at last.
You'd swear there was no such thing as the past.
But the past is there, it keeps its life
In spite of house and child and wife.

Now what do you think of this for gumption!
Says the Lover to me, 'Moloney, old pal, will you
Do me a favour? When I go to her house
To pop the question
I want her to see the two of us
There on the doorstep. I'll be dressed
Like a lord, much better than best.
I want you to act as my serving-man
To whom I will hand my hat and cane
When she opens the door.' 'All right,' I said,
Thinkin' of her he'd lured from my bed.
'Lover, old pal, you have your man
Ready to take your hat and cane,
Willin' to go through flood and fire

To see that you get your heart's desire.'

The day arrived. We approached her house,
The lordly Lover and my humble self,
Bearing his hat and stick. A few yards from the door
The Lover said, 'Hand me my topper now.'
I did, and he put it on his head
As I knocked at the door which she opened
Herself. The Lover smiled from ear to ear
And doffed his hat with a flourish there.
As he did, she screamed in fright
Or perhaps in disgust at the sight
Of the shite on the Lover's head
Sittin' there, innocent, neat,
Till it plopped to the ground at the girl's feet
From the polished head of the Lover Flynn.
The Lover's face was black as sin
As he whirled on me but I was the one
Who was laughin' now after sweet revenge
Well taken. Triumphant now and ready to run
I spoke to my lord
A few simple words -
'Lover, old pal, what's the use,' I said,
'Of love in your heart if you've shit on your head?'
And then I was gone. Revenge was sweet.
The Lover's future stank as his feet.
The sound of my laugh was the sound of the past
Squaring accounts with the Lover at last.

MOLONEY
RECALLS
THE
MARRIAGE
OF THE
BARRELL
MULDOON

The Barrell Muldoon, Moloney said,
  Was eighty-two when he married
A wife. The Barrell owned a farm o' land
And carried success in the palm o' his hand;
Sat on his money like a bird in the nest,
The young flock under the wing. The best
Thing a man can do, the Barrell would say,
Is to bide his time and wait for the day
When 'tis ripe to consider a wife,
Somewhere near the tail-end of his life.
Then catch her young, own her body and soul,
Treat her rough, tell her nothin' at all.
But don't be too hasty, he'd add. Time enough
For all the midnight sport o' love
And in any case I've heard it stated
This thing called love is over-rated.

  The Barrell kept his word.
At eighty-two, he took the third
Daughter of a labourin' man,
A slight little queen
Of a thing,
Barely sixteen,
But with a flash in her eye that late or soon
Would change the tune
Of the Barrell Muldoon.

  You'd think she'd show disgust at the notion
Of losin' her flower to an old man's passion.

You'd think she'd scream, or shrink, or spit.
Was she bothered? - Divil a bit!

As creatures go, Moloney said,
There's none as odd
As a woman.
Enough to puzzle the mind o' God.
If a woman puzzles the God that made her
How can a poor man understand her?

Anyway, as the Barrell has said,
He got the girl in the bridal bed
And mounted up. You won't believe it! At eighty-two
The Barrell hardly knew what to do.

There he was near the end of his life
Astride his sweet little child of a wife,
Pleased with himself, like a buyer at an auction,
But hardly able to get an erection.
I'll help you, Barrell, the girl said,
And started to pass
Her fingers up and down his arse
Which,
After eighty-two years of Irish weather
Was tough and cold as cobbler's leather.

At this, the Barrell started to laugh.
Stop it, he said, if you tickle my arse
I can't perform with the length of laughin'.

O ever since the cradle, he cried,
The most sensitive part o' me is my backside,
So stop your ticklin' straightaway,
And, ha-ha-ha, pray, girl, pray
That my drooped, discouraged johnny will stand
And do his duty at my command.

But the slight little queen
Kept on passin' her fingers up and down
The Barrell's hindquarters. In no time at all
The Barrell was laughin' like a fool,
Eager to love, unable to quit,
Tremblin' in his laughin' fit,
His old body shakin' all over,
A helpless, ridiculous, quiverin' lover,
Till, honest to God, he stiffened in bed
And fell off his bride, dead
To the world and the job in hand.
With staring eyes and open gob,
The Barrell Muldoon died on the job,
Not the first oul' shagger to die on duty,
Tickled to death by an innocent beauty.

The slight little queen got a terrible fright,
Having lost her man on the very first night.
She got over it though, and
Shortly after, she took a man.
Husband and wife on the Barrell's farm,
They reared a family of ten

Who grew up to be solid women and men
All because the slight little queen,
Full of the tricks of sweet sixteen,
On the very first night of her honeymoon
Tickled the arse of the Barrell Muldoon.

MOLONEY
CURES
THE
CURSE

A short dickey is a terrible curse,
Moloney said, I doubt if there's worse
Can torment a man. A small
Farmer two miles outside Listowel
Found that his dickey never grew
And the poor hoor hardly knew what to do.
God between us and every harm
He'd mope like an eejit round the farm
Prayin' to God his dickey would grow
But divil a bit did it grow and so
The farmer decided to go to Lourdes
To see would a miracle do the trick
But the longer the prayer the shorter the dick
And back he came to the awful plight
Of empty days and lonesome nights.

Now, as our mothers often told us,
Every Christian has his cross
And this particular farmer's was
The shy little fella between his thighs
Causin' him endless misery.
When I heard of his case, I decided to go
And tell him the only thing I knew
Might cure him. A widdawoman from Knockanore
Had a name for curin' rich and poor
Of every ailment that plagues mankind,
Sickness of body and of mind,
Warts, measles, goitre, gripe,
Pains in the belly, balls and back,

Madness, badness, sadness too,
Whatever bores us black and blue,
Carbuncles, boils, blockin' of wind,
Shaky bones that once were sound,
Women whose milk is known to be sour,
Men who are scourged by the yella scour,
Scurvy blackheads as black as rocks,
Nightmares, nosebleeds, gout and pox,
Piles in the arse, pains in the head
And misfortune caused by watery blood.
Only one thing the patient must have for sure -
Faith in the widda's power to cure.
You can imagine my farmer was ready
To trust in any hopeful body.

     Well, I took him straightaway
To her. Slippin' off his pants without delay
She said she'd do her best to grow
A weapon he'd always be proud to show
To the world, and then and there she
Rubbed his Charley tenderly
As a loving mother caresses a child
Who looks like he might grow up to be wild.
A lively look was in her eyes
And she said as she stroked and patted too -
'I think I see a future for you.
Your grief is gone, your joy assured,
A man o' your faith is bound to be cured.
Faith is what poor Adam cried for.

Faith is what your ancestors died for.
Faith is the power that makes all thing grow
Between God above and the Devil below!'

She never said a truer word.
Whatever she did the next I heard
Was that the farmer and the widda were
Walkin' together up to the altar
To be joined forever in holy wedlock.
Whatever she did to the farmer's cock
The proof was there inside a year
Bawlin' and cryin' in both their ears.

Some people think
She gave him tarwater to drink.
Others say she fed him on pills for weeks.
But I'd swear to God the secret lay
In the way her eyes lit up that day.
When she touched his boyo it started to swell
And from that moment all was well.
So my conclusion, Moloney said,
Is if dickeys are short and times are bad
And a man is forgotten by heaven on high,
Find a woman with light in her eye;
Trust in her knowledge of muscles and glands
And leave the future in her hands.
Faith in faith is faith indeed
But faith in a woman is all we need.

MOLONEY REMEMBERS TIMMY THANKGOD

Timmy Thankgod, a respectable man, Moloney said,
Kicked the bucket when the weather turned bad.
Timmy was named for the habit he had
Of offerin' thanks to the heavenly God
Every minute and hour o' the day
For whatever advantage came his way.
If he sold a calf, he'd close his eyes
And liftin' his face to the silent sky,
Say, 'Thank you, thank you, thank you, God,'
And slip the money into his pocket.
If a brown penny made him feel good
He'd storm heaven with gratitude.
But he died at last on a winter's night
And I was there to lay him out.
                    After he died,
He was twisted and crumpled up in the bed,
His mouth agape, his legs astray, his head
Hangin' out over the side, limp
As a fish on a river's bank. I
Straightened him up without delay
And called his wife, Maynanne, to have
The boilin' water ready to shave
The black stubble from his face.
Maynanne was flyin' all over the place,
Worried to death after losin' her man
Who had always offered thanks to God
For favours received. But to give her her due,
She got the kettle o' boilin' water for me.
With an open razor in my hand

I shaved the face of Timmy Thankgod.

'Sweet Jesus, Moloney,' said Maynanne,
'You're wan dacent Christian man
To put yourself out like that for me.'
'Maynanne,' said I,
"Tis a privilege. Any man should have
The pleasure of a last shave,
And if you look at your husband's body
You'll agree that he's lookin' better already.'
She looked, and with wonder in her eyes,
'He's better now than ever he was,'
She said, 'Twenty years a younger man,
And when he's rigged out in his habit,
                    he'll be younger again.
I have no doubt but that he'll be
As handsome as the day he married me.'

            There and then,
With Maynanne gone out, I stripped my man
Ballsnaked to put his habit on.
'Twas made of the best material,
The kind of stuff that'll wear well
Even in the grave where fashion
Is not important for men and women.
After strippin' him, I got the surprise
O' my life. I could hardly believe my eyes.
The naked corpse of Timmy Thankgod
Lay there before me on the bed.

What rattled me though was that Timmy had got
A small bag tied round his you-know-what,
As neat as ever you'd wish to see,
Innocent as the flowers o' May.
Very delicately I untied
The bag and looked inside.
A feather would knock me on the ground
As I counted out five hundred pounds
In fifty-pound notes. I looked at my man, dead
As yesterday's love in the bed
And I thought, No wonder, Timmy, that you could
Be always offerin' thanks to God
And finish your days, pious and cute,
With a bag o' money tied to your flute,
Grateful to God for life's poor dregs
With the Bank of Ireland between your legs.
But I'm not the man to find
Fault with you. Far from it. It takes every kind
To make up the world o' men
And I'll not say who's right and who's wrong
So long as I've time for a drink and a song
Because I am blind, O Christ how I'm blind
And ignorant of what the next minute will find.

The next minute, I called Maynanne
And gave her half the cash in her fist.
I said, 'Good woman, be grateful to Christ,'
'I am, I am,' she cried, 'Oh
Tell me where it came from, though.'

'Maynanne,' I said, 'Be grateful for what
God has given you. That's all you've got.
That money is from the very source of life.'
'O wisha,' she said, 'don't addle me. I'm a wife
No longer, but a widda in black
Compelled to suffer alone every knock and shock
That life can offer.' 'Never mind,' I said,
'Although he's stretched and shaved and dead
Your husband was a Christian man
And will leave you enough to see you through.'
Her eyes were glad. 'Moloney, you know,
He was fond of his ha'penny, but in his way
He was always thinkin' of me, maybe.
And now I must plant him under the sod.
Thank God,' sighed the widow of Timmy Thankgod.

Moloney
and
the
Dust

B efore Mike Nelligan died, Moloney said,
   He willed that he wanted to be cremated
And to have every grain of his mortal dust
Scattered abroad in the Shannon. He asked
Me once, since I was his friend,
If I'd scatter him to the Shannon wind.
I thought for a while 'twas fearful odd
But there's many a way to go to God
And this was as good as any. Nelligan, I said,
I'll be glad to scatter you after you're dead!

Years later, Mike Nelligan died
An' I arranged to have him cremated.
At death he weighed over sixteen stone
But when the burnin' was done
Nelligan fitted in a small box
That I tucked away in my arse-pocket,
As fine a dust as could blow your way
When the wind plays games of a summer's day.

Well, I hired a boat at Tarbert Quay
And rowed out into the Shannon
Till I was a fair distance from the land.
Then I stopped, pulled in the oars,
Stood up in the boat and looked around.
Not a sinner in sight except myself
And a mangy seagull overhead.
The day was as good as you'd hope to find
Except for a tricky Shannon wind.

I looked around for another minute,
Then I took Mike Nelligan out o' my pocket.
With a final look at the dust o' the dead
I pitched it high above my head.
It seemed for a moment to stick in the air
As if 'twould linger forever there
But that tricky hoor of a Shannon wind
Blew it straight back into my mouth
And I swear to God before I could tell
What had happened, I could feel
The dust slippin' down my throat
And not a thing I could do about it.
It took me several minutes to see
Exactly what had happened to me.
In the blink of an eye, after all my pains,
I had swallowed Mike Nelligan's mortal remains
Or a large part o' them, anyway.

For a while, as I'm sure you'll understand,
I thought I'd go clean out of my mind.
I'm not the kind to swallow a friend.
But then I thought what I had to think.
I'll go back to Tarbert for a drink
And pray for the peace of Nelligan's soul.
What does it matter after all
Where the dead will come to rest -
In seas no human heart has blessed?
Hacked fields of awful wars?
Mockin' faces of the stars?

Or it may happen that the dead are blown
Back in the guts of a livin' man.
Through fire or water, sane or mad,
There's many a way to go to God.
And why should it matter how a man will go?
That Shannon wind will always blow.

Without further delay, with peace of mind,
I started to row me back to land.
One mangy seagull in the sky
Was all I had for company
Till I stood in a pub in Tarbert town
And washed my good friend Nelligan down.
Mike Nelligan's dust and Arthur Guinness
Mingled happily within me.
'God rest you, Mike,' I said as I drank,
Thinking how fire had made him shrink,
'God rest your dust in river and sea
And God rest the rest of your dust in me.'

MOLONEY
REMEMBERS
THE
RESURRECTION
OF
KATE
FINUCANE

O she was the handsome corpse, he said,
Divil a difference between livin' and dead
You'd see in her; a fine red face
On a starchy pillow edged with lace,
Her cold hands clasped, her mousy hair
As neatly tied as a girl's at a fair.
Touchin' forty she was when she passed away,
But twenty she looked as she lay
In bed on the broad of her back.
Kate Finucane of Asdee West
Was stretched in death, but she looked her best!

       Her cousins had come
From all parts of the Kingdom
For the wake; Coffeys and Lanes from Dingle,
McCarthys and Ryans, married and single,
Honest and otherwise. For a day and a night
As she lay in her bed, a sight
For sore eyes, they drank and they prayed
And they sang her to heaven - as fine
A wake as ever I went to in all my time!

Well, there was nothin' to do, after prayin' and drinkin',
But lift herself into the coffin.
'Twas at that moment, glory to God,
As I stood with my glass at the head
Of her bed, that she stretched like a cat
       and opened her eyes
And lifted her head in great surprise;

And motherogod will I ever forget
The cut an' the go, the sight an' the set
Of her when, calm as you like, with a toss of her head,
Kate Finucane sat up in the bed!

   No need to tell
Of all the commotion that fell
On the cousins, neighbours, myself and the house.
Dead she'd been, and now this disastrous
Return to life, upsettin' the whole
Place, and I thinkin' her body was lackin' a soul.
But after a while, things quietened down
And Kate made tea for the cousins. She found
She'd not seen them for ages. What's more,
She clapped her eye on a Lenamore
Man called Harty, and three months later,
Paraded him in rare style up to the altar!
On top o' that, she showed the world she could
Make a dandy wife, for she's still to the good,
And without doubt or favour, fright or fear,
Kate Finucane has a child a year!

Gay woman, Kate, Moloney said
Divil a difference between livin' and dead!

MOLONEY
ENTERS
INTO A
DIALOGUE
CONCERNING
THE
LISTOWEL
WATER
SUPPLY

D id you ever know, Moloney said,
      That half the genius of Europe
Is found in Listowel
An' thereabouts?
Many's the time I stood in that town
And threw a cautious look around
Wonderin' how, between sane an' mad,
So many were riddled with the light o' God.

    And then, one day, in that same Listowel,
Weary in body and in soul,
I was drinkin' whiskey in a pub
(Nothin' like it to warm the guts)
And chattin' with the publican's daughter.
I asked her for a drop o' water
To put in the whiskey. She turned the tap
An' gave me the water in a glass.
The water was the colour o' clay.
The girl said nothin'. I didn't know what to say
At first, an' then - 'Tell me, girl, how is it
That the water here is coloured like that?'
'Moloney,' she said, 'I wish my father were here
To instruct you about the Listowel water
But he's gone to a funeral in Asdee West
To bury that woman, Kate Finucane.
'Tis up to me to do my best
So I'll answer your question as good as I can.
Sometimes the water is the colour o' mud
An' moretimes reddish, blackish, brown.

That's the water we drink in town.'
'My God,' I replied, 'Do you mean to say
You drink coloured water every day?'
'O we do,' she said, 'As a matter of fact
I often wonder what colour is next -
Brown or green or black or red
Or yella like under a nanny-goat's tail!'
'But water shouldn't be coloured,' I said,
'Anyone livin' will tell you that.'
As cool as you like - 'Moloney,' she said,
'The coloured water you have in your glass
Flows through the graveyard near the town.
If you don't believe me you can kiss my arse.
That's why the water is yella and brown,
Green, pink, red and orange too,
French mustard, amber, and royal blue.
Here in Listowel, Moloney, you'll find
All the colours of God's own mind.'

I was dumb as a corpse but after a bit
I managed at last to gather my wits.
'Do you mean to tell me, girl,' I said,
'This water flows through the bones o' the dead
And that every one o' the Listowel scuts
Drinks his ancestors into his guts
In coloured water, dazzlin' the sight?
O holymotherojaysus tonight!'

Up spoke the girl with an innocent wink,
'Doesn't it bate Moll Bell to think
That when a Listowel man takes a drink
From any tap in this lovely town
'Tis not only water that's goin' down
But the purified secrets of the dead
Flowin' into his belly and through his head.
No town here or in any land
Will do this for your body an' mind.
No wonder MacMahon, for all his sins,
Will riddle you a story that spins.
And John B. Keane, when the water is right,
Is able to write a play a night.
Sure even that fat little bollox
Out in Ballylongford, Kennelly,
Is half-able to write
With a drop o' Listowel water in his belly.
Not, mind you, that he'd ever produce
Anything as original as this.
The poor bastard is too serious,
When he's not foolish he's delirious.
Inspiration flows through the graveyard sod,
Turn a tap in Listowel; out flows God.

'Mister Moloney,' the girl said,
'Who'd think there was such life in the dead?
Not many give the dead a thought or
Bit of attention, but here we have 'em in the water.
I swear to you, upon my soul,

Genius is common in Listowel
An' thereabouts.'

   'I can see that,' I replied,
'Isn't it time all Ireland tried
The coloured water in Listowel.
Quick as it takes to empty a glass
Stupidity would quit the land.
We'd all be able to think and then
The fools o' the land would be clever men.'

   'In that case, Mister Moloney,' she smiled
As if she could decipher the world
And everything in it,
'The water just now is royal blue,
The right colour for a man like you.
So pour it into your whiskey now
And the light of heaven will visit your brow.'

   I looked at that water, Moloney said,
An' I saw the wisdom of the dead
There for the drinkin'. But I'm sorry that I
Was born a coward, and a coward I'll die.
A fool I am, a fool I'll remain,
For the likes o' me, what good is a brain?
Like a shot, my hand went for the glass
And in one quick gulp I knocked it back.
'Cheerio,' I said to the publican's daughter,
'I prefer my whiskey without any water.'